60 70 80 90

Planning ahead for satisfying senior years

David C. Pratt

Philip Garside Publishing Ltd.

ISBN 978-1-927260-16-6

Philip Garside Publishing Ltd
PO Box 17160
Wellington 6147
New Zealand

books@pgpl.co.nz   www.pgpl.co.nz

Front cover design: Aaron Courtney

Printed by CreateSpace

Available on Kindle and other retail outlets

Contents

Dedication

When I consider growing old I often think of my grandmother, Mabel Selleck. 'Ma,' as we affectionately called her, died in 1969 aged 93. I was a young man aged 26 just beginning my chosen career. Ma was often in our home, sometimes shared camping holidays with us and was a significant person in our family. I did not realise until recently, as I began to experience old age myself, just how much influence she had on my upbringing. I learned from her that there is an essential wisdom that is carried by those old in years and wise in experience. It is the task of senior people to share that wisdom, to pass it on to those younger, those who are becoming older. What Ma passed to me, and a little of my experience of growing old, I gladly share.

Foreword

I consider that my best work has been among people my own age. I realised this when, as a parent with three young children, I became interested in children's development. Then as I grew older I became involved in helping seniors live well.

I write as a result of that experience, but I also write because I have begun the old age journey myself, and I am beginning to understand how important it is to grasp the opportunities that old age offers us to shape life well.

For many years I worked as a hospital chaplain. A large part of my work involved listening to the stories of people growing older, people who were finding that they had to adjust their lifestyle to suit their years. I count it a privilege to have heard their stories and to have shared their insights.

In 2006 I was forced by my own medical condition to retire a few months early. It was then that I really began to understand personally what aging was all about. Nothing had prepared me for this experience. I had lived imagining that I would continue to be healthy and fit and somehow adjust to living on a smaller income. The reality for me was quite different. I began to realise that the adjustment required from full employment to retirement was huge, requiring both physical and mental processes.

Often in old people I met my grandmother again. I was reminded of her complaints about the uneven surface holes in footpaths. Ma walked everywhere. We used to smile at her complaints. But she was quite right about the footpaths, and the situation has not changed. My illness means that I am no longer permitted to drive a car so I now walk everywhere or take a bus. (I shall forever be thankful for free senior's bus rides.) And it is true, the footpaths are full of sudden surprises for those who can no longer lift their feet high enough as they walk. I will not forget the first time I fell in the street. Some Chinese students had stopped me to ask directions to an English Language School. I was able to help them, but as I turned to continue on uphill I tripped and fell in the gutter. That gave them the opportunity to very graciously help me. Only my ego was a little bruised.

I recall on many occasions saying, "I wish someone had written explaining that old age would have its difficulties, its pain and frustration, written to point out the pitfalls and possibilities of the way ahead." On one occasion I shared this thought with the hospital manager. Her immediate response was, "Why don't you write it?" Well here it is. And it's not all pain and pitfalls.

I hope that what I have written is not too disturbing, for old age can be trying; it can really test our patience. But it can also be full of rich moments, new insights, much laughter and enjoyment; often about small occurrences and simple memories.

The Auckland Savings Bank many years ago used this jingle in their advertising to attract elderly customers, "The best is yet to be." How right they were.

Getting Started

Phyllis will be 102 in May. When she is not resting in her La-Z-Boy chair, Phyllis shares memories of growing up as a child in pre-First World War New Zealand. It is a privilege to hear her story. When Phyllis was 100 the Queen and the Prime Minister sent her letters of congratulation. Her family gathered, we blew up balloons and we cut a birthday cake. 100 is a significant milestone. In the past few people reached that mark. Now people are living longer and the Queen is quite busy writing letters.

We may not live until we reach 100, but a good number of us born since the Second World War will reach 80. Certainly there will come a day when you wish to retire from an active working life. Age creeps up on us, and before we know it, we are aged 65 and receiving National Superannuation. We all know that this day will come. In NZ retirement opportunities usually come at age 65. Retirement is not really the right word; to cease full time paid work is a better description. Many retirees find just as much to do in their so called retirement as they did when fully employed.

Retirement can have many benefits and opportunities. I felt that retirement meant that I could now say, "Yes" or "No" when asked to do a job. Instead of having to be shaped by the job, its timetable and its pay structure, I could now shape each day as I chose. The necessity to have an income no longer applied, as I now receive NZ Superannuation. I no longer observe office hours; I have no office. Neither is there a contract to which I must work.

If you live in a society that has a culture of measuring worth by financial reward for work done, by time spent at work and by observing and keeping contracts and commitments, as we do, then the transition to retirement offers a very significant change of lifestyle.

We are trained by repetitive work habits and years of timetabling. Our body clock tells us when we should wake and when we should eat. I habitually wake at 6.30am on the dot, even though I have been retired for six years. But I now lie in bed for half an hour before rising. During that half hour and the minutes following, when I enjoy a warm shower, I sort out in my mind what I will do that day. I have found in my retirement that

I like to achieve something significantly useful or creative each day. Perhaps giving some thought to tomorrow is a good way to end the day. Letting a thought simmer in the mind overnight often allows that thought to be sorted by the morning.

If retirement has meant a significant drop in income, money matters become quite demanding. That probably describes most of us. Planning well ahead and keeping to a strict budget helps make the money go round. (See Finance and money matters)

At age 60 plus most of us begin to think about retiring. In NZ the Government National Superannuation scheme pays those aged 65 and over a significant living wage. Consequently, at about age 60 we begin to think seriously about planning our retirement at 65. Therein is a problem — five years are not long enough to address all the issues involved, and to take all the steps necessary to ensure a smooth transition to retirement. Neither are five years of planning and saving time enough to ensure that we have the financial wherewithal to continue our present and expected standard of living and lifestyle. Neither do five years allow us enough time to plan activities that will match our physical and mental capabilities, activities that will offer us a sense of significant fulfilment in retirement.

Probably the ideal time to start planning for retirement is the day we start work. But retirement and old age are the last things on our mind, at a time when everything is new and exciting, and we have the prospects of an income and a big wide world to explore. Another opportunity comes about 25 years later when our youngest child leaves home. We get a second chance to adjust our lifestyle. Many do make significant changes, but many of us fail to begin the long term adjustments that will be necessary if we are to shape a fulfilling retirement. For some this after-family opportunity comes as early as age 45 or 50. But once again, there are so many other exciting things to choose from: a new car, travel, getting involved and more committed to an interest, an activity or a community service. The reality that right NOW is the best time to plan ahead for old age, once again evades us. Too often our mindset says, "There is plenty of time for that later." Then suddenly we are 60 and we realise that "later" has arrived. NOW is the time. Right now it is time to address all the questions and make a raft of decisions that will shape the next 25 years.

Questions that we should address may need to include:

- When is the best time for me to retire?
- Do I want to change my career or lifestyle?
- Are there things I want to do before I retire?
- Will I want to retrain or learn a new skill?
- Will our 60 plus lifestyle be suited to our present home?
- Is our home well located?
- What sort of transport will we need?
- Do household appliances need replacing?
- Household pets: Yes or No?
- Is my health able to support my dreams?
- Will our income support our retirement lifestyle?
- Is my present partner included?
- Do my beliefs compliment my lifestyle?

Often the questions to be answered are small; there are a thousand details to determine. But many of these small questions turn out to be quite significant. Small issues may have a considerable influence on other aspects of our retirement and together determine our retirement lifestyle. The next few pages deal with some of these issues.

Where will we live?

Home is where the heart is. Home is where we feel that we can be ourselves. It is where we feel free to bring our friends and where conversation and ideas are shared. Home is where our inner-self is nurtured and our being is respected. It is where we are able to rest, but also where we are often most creative. Home is where we dream and where dreams come to fruition. It is where we can laugh, where we can cry and where our hurts are healed. Home is where we are loved and where we love in return. It is where our soul is happy to live.

Where is home? That's a deep question, and may take considerable time and thought to answer. Perhaps we are quite happy to drift on living where we have always lived. Perhaps that is where we are most 'at home.' If you have lived and worked in the one town or city, one locality, most of your life, home will probably be right there among friends and family.

For those whose job provided a house, and for those whose work often promoted them by shifting them to another location, the question "Where is home?" becomes very real. Farmers are a good example of those whose work location provided them with a home. Retirement may mean for them the upheaval of leaving the residence they have occupied all their working life, while their son, or a new owner, takes over the farm business. School teachers, ministers of religion and a host of government workers face similar situations. Retirement means for them the upheaval of relocating. For such people retirement may mean leaving their friends and the community to which they have contributed, and which shaped their living throughout their working life.

One of the most important facets of your decisions regarding your retirement location may well be the question: "Where do my friends and family live, and do I want to be near them?" If they are scattered far and wide you may find it difficult to choose your location. The choice may well come down to, "With which of my children and grandchildren do I have the most rapport?" Other questions may be, "How much time do I expect to have to myself?" and, "Do I want to be looking after grandchildren every day after school?" Consider also, "Do I want to spend a lot of time in my car driving to visit those I love?" Then there is the question, "I've

10

got friends and relatives all over the world. If I want travel, how much time will I spend at home?"

Health issues may influence your chosen retirement location. If you need to be near doctors and a hospital, then you need a home in the city. Consider your interests. You love trees and gardens. On the other hand, you can't stand having a large lawn that needs weekly mowing. Make your choices taking into account your needs likes and dislikes. Remember that no location will be 100% perfect.

It will help to have the understanding support of your immediate family when you make this important decision. Talk with your children before you finalise anything and hear how they view your retirement dreams and intentions. But do not let them make decisions for you that you do not fully understand and agree with. The decision about where you will live is yours, not theirs, to make.

Most of us have a handful of close friends whom we can really trust. It may help to talk with them as well. It depends upon how close you are to your friends. If you are the transport provider for a small group, or have weekly café meetings and share meals regularly with your friends, you are not going to be very happy to move far at all. If you've met daily on the bowling green for the past ten years, you will not want to suddenly break up the team.

Interests of a lifetime have to be considered. The model railway enthusiast will not want to be far from the clubhouse with its track layout. Neither will the committed Church or lodge member lightly make a move which will end their ability to continue that commitment.

Consider the effort of making new contacts, finding another doctor, moving away from the chiropractor, and those who provided all the services you have enjoyed and come to rely upon — dentist, bank, garage mechanic, electrician — the list is endless. All these can be replaced if you relocate, but are the hassles worth the effort?

Fortunately there are some alternatives. I've already suggested that you could become a traveller. Scan the travel sites and advertisements and search for the discounted fares.

In this electronic age of fast connections you could become a Skype expert. Set up your computer so that you can talk to and see your family and grandchildren on a weekly or daily basis. Skype uses the Internet, not the telephone system, so it is relatively cheap. You will need a small video camera and have to install a copy of the free Skype programme. If you already have a computer you can, for an outlay of less than $100, acquire the gear you need to regularly share, and video conference with, anyone who also has acquired Skype, anywhere in the world.

A note of caution. I have known couples who in their retirement have moved several times, never seeming to settle. On each occasion their capital has been further reduced by land agents fees, removal costs and the inevitable minor costs of transferring accounts and obtaining services, telephone, banking, doctor, etc. The basic problem is that they in themselves are unsettled people. Take a good look at yourself. Have good reasons for moving, before you make the final decision. And make sure that when you decide to move, you plan your move thoroughly. Perhaps people who make several moves have not thought far enough ahead about their needs, their health and their diminishing energy levels. Think carefully, and think again, before making far reaching decisions that you may later regret. Relocation is a serious and expensive business.

Home: The house we live in

Henry Van Dyke tells the story of *The Other Wise Man.* Artiban, as a young man seeking adventure, sells all that he owns, buys three jewels, and sets off to join the three wise men following the star to Bethlehem. Helping a wounded Hebrew on the road results in him missing the appointed meeting place. The three wise men journey on without Artiban. He, in his lonely journey following the star, is distracted time and time again, pausing to help those in need. At Bethlehem, while the newborn are slaughtered, he hides a mother and baby, bribing a soldier with one of his jewels to leave them alone. There is a slave girl whose ransom is paid. After 30 years journeying, helping others and seeking the Christ, Artiban's jewels are spent. At the Hill of Golgotha, Artiban, as an old man with nothing left to give, feels the despair of the Christ and weeps at his own failure. It is then that he hears the quiet words of the Christ, "In as much as you did it for one of the least of these my children, you did it for me."

Sometimes the way we choose does not take the turnings we might have expected. We travel in directions we had not dreamt of taking and end up living where we had not planned to live. Perhaps deciding how to live is a more important question than deciding where to live. The other wise man was such a person.

When you have decided how and where to live, it is time to consider the actual home in which you will live. Will it meet your on going retirement needs? And, given that you will probably be living there for the next two decades, your choice of home needs to match your lifestyle and your physical abilities.

If you want to stay put, is your present home a satisfactory match to your aging body? Do you always want to be climbing stairs to the bedroom and bathroom? We once owned a home with the kitchen and living area on the first floor. It had a great view. But we soon got tired of climbing and carrying everything upstairs. Do you have too much lawn to mow yourself? When does the place next need a paint job? Then there are all those small maintenance jobs that need doing. Who will carry out these tasks? Do you have the energy to do all these things?

Some adjustments and alterations may be necessary to adapt your home to your advancing years. Perhaps you need a ramp for easier access instead of steps. Bathrooms and toilets can be fitted with grab rails which may prevent unwanted falls. Get rid of floor rugs which have the potential to trip you up. Install a clothes dryer so that you don't have to hang out washing. An automatic robotic vacuum cleaner will save you from that energy consuming task of vacuum cleaning regularly. Sort out the bathroom, get rid of the bath and install a good shower. Buy a plastic stool so that you can sit in the shower. Organise storage space that allows you to get regularly used items without climbing or reaching.

Maybe your home is located on a road that has become a busy highway. Do you always want to live with traffic noise and congestion? Will driving out of your entrance become a problem? You may find it more helpful to be located near a shopping mall, medical care, easily accessed transport or a library. You originally bought the property because it was near the school. Your children have long since become adults with families of their own. Your needs and requirements are now quite different.

Size does matter. Do you still need four bedrooms, or could you live more comfortably in a two bedroom apartment? Perhaps you need the extra room for all those mementoes of what used to be? Or maybe you need the extra room for when all the family come home at Christmas? Alternatively, could it be time that you started going to your family each Christmas?

Downsizing to a more suitable home can have benefits, but it may also come with its problems. There will be less wall space. "Where will I hang treasured family photographs?" Have those reminders of overseas travel become little more than dust collectors? The children's school artwork and all the handmade Christmas and birthday cards. Has the time come to discard these memories of the past? The chair that I have loved to relax in each evening; and Dad's chair, I can't just throw them away. But they are too big for my downsized lounge-kitchen-dining room. "I wish I could keep the piano, but my daughter says it has to go." The questions, the decisions and the emotions are almost overwhelming. Downsizing, even shifting house, can be very stressful.

Perhaps you should ask yourself some questions about your house and your health. Disabilities sometimes mean that our present home becomes unsuitable. Is there adequate room to manoeuvre a walking frame? Can I bend enough to plug appliances into the power points? Can I still hang out the washing? (This becomes an extraordinarily difficult task if you have to use a walking frame.) Would a shower be more suitable than a bath, or should I go really modern and have the bathroom converted into a wet room? Are there too many steps and stairs? Do the steps at both front and back doors hinder me going in and out of the house?

There is another sense in which size does matter. Cities and towns are becoming more compact as people choose to live closer to the services that they require. As a consequence it has become popular to subdivide the back yard, build a unit and sell off the house. Often the result is a much more suitable retirement home. If planned and executed well, the costs may be fully met by the sale of the front property. This may be a better option than staying in the family home. You may also find that your rates are lower, and that you have less grass to mow and garden to weed. It pays to do your homework well before choosing this option.

Retirement villages

It is possible, and many choose this option, to sell your home, and for about the same capital outlay, buy your way into a unit at a retirement village. This option gives you a brand new apartment and often it comes with shared community facilities, a bowling green, a swimming pool, a café, a restaurant, and sometimes a workshop or sewing room. It is upmarket accommodation. The gardener keeps the lawns and gardens. Someone cleans your windows and sweeps the paths and corridors. There may be bridge afternoons, a coffee club, free newspapers and a library. For some this is a good option. It allows you to choose a balance between being independent and being close to those who can help you if you need help.

There are retirement village opportunities where you can have your own small garden to grow vegetables and flowers. These units are often more costly. Each retirement village has its own characteristics and offers a range of options from which to choose.

Sounds like heaven. There is a monthly cost involved, the body corporate fee, which is used to service and maintain common areas. You will be surrounded by older people who are aging. This will not provide a daily balance of young and old, particularly children, in your life. This option is not for those who wish to have a substantial vegetable garden, build a boat or construct their own furniture. But it is the choice of many and there is a high level of satisfaction among those who choose the retirement village lifestyle.

Any move to a retirement village must be your choice. Your family should not make such a far reaching decision on your behalf without your full consent. You will have strong thoughts and preferences. Make sure that your ideas are discussed and heard by them. But the choice must be yours, for you are the one who has to live with the results of what is a most important decision.

The organisation Guide to Retirement Living has published a directory of that name which lists opportunities available for living in a retirement home or village. Their contact details are in the appendix *Organisations Working with Older People.*

Consider the option of building a new home

For many this will not be an option at all. But if you have looked forward to a new home in your retirement, read on. This is an option for those who have the capital to do so. The last thing you want in your retirement is to be tied to the repayment of a mortgage. Have a very careful look at your savings and the worth of your present home before you proceed.

Also consider your health. Are you fit enough to live with the stress involved in building a new home? After a heart attack, new home construction is the biggest killer of senior people. It can be a very risky and stressful road to travel.

The easiest way to a new home, if this option is for you, is to buy a new home. Find a real estate agent who will listen to your requirements and you will get all the assistance you need.

If you do decide to build a home, have a look at the housing companies who will have a range of pre-designed homes for you to consider. With some housing companies you can make minor alterations to the basic floor plan. With others you will be able to choose fittings, carpets, paint schemes and other minor small items. The advantage of working with such companies is that they will be able to give you a time frame. You will know when you can move in and you will be able to time your relocation to suit your needs.

Then there is the option of designing and building your own home. Very few will want to actually construct their new home themselves. For most it is essential to employ a builder. Ask around and look at the construction and finish of other new homes before you make your choice. You may be wise to employ an architect to design your home. That way all the details will be given adequate thought. But architects are costly. Determine the cost of an architect before you commit. Make sure that whoever designs your home knows your dreams and your wishes. If you want a large master bedroom, say so. If you want huge windows to let in as much light as possible, say so. Will you be doing a fair bit of entertaining? Let the architect know that you want a large kitchen, dining room and lounge. Go through every detail before the first spade of earth is turned. Know what you are paying for and make sure that you get it.

A multitude of questions need to be worked through before you commit to building new. Let's list some of them. (These are also the characteristics that you would be wise to consider if you are buying your retirement home.)

- How many rooms? How many bedrooms? Will you often have guests or family staying?

- Will you need a work room, study or office? Will this also fulfil the purpose of an extra bedroom?

- There should be at least one bedroom downstairs on the living level. If you become unwell or disabled this will save you from continually climbing stairs.

- How many toilets will you require? It has become the norm to have one downstairs and a guest toilet near the guest bedroom and bathroom.

- Will the bathroom contain a toilet and shower? Or will it be a wet room — a room with a waterproof floor and a shower in one corner? The advantages are that there will be no steps to trip over as the floor will be on one level and it will be easier to clean. Do you need a bath? Make sure that any separate toilet room is large enough for those with stiff limbs and joints to negotiate.

- A storage room is a great idea. Such a room lined with shelving should be built in every home.

- Hallways need to be wide enough for a wheelchair and doors need to be easily opened. Consider sliding cavity doors in suitable places.

- There should ideally be no steps and stairs. Entrance and exit points should be flat with nothing to trip over. Easy flow to porches decks and back yards is important. Consider a ramp instead of steps. Make sure that there is wheelchair access.

- Have plenty of power points and have them set at levels that require little bending and reaching. You can never have too many.

- Have plenty of adequate lighting, especially in areas where you work in the evenings at some craft, or where you get comfortable to read a book or newspaper. Remember that aged eyesight sometimes deteriorates. Good lighting always helps.

- Tiled floors look good but are most unforgiving if you fall. No one wants a broken limb in old age.

- Choose the colour scheme of walls and carpets wisely. You do have to think about resale value.

- Kitchen cupboards must be accessible without too much bending or climbing.

- Make sure that there is adequate kitchen bench space. How many appliances do you need to accommodate?

- Fridge and freezer will need easy access. Do you need a separate freezer?

- What sized range and hob do you really need?

- Will the pantry be large enough?

- Do you want separate kitchen, dining and lounge rooms, or will these be open plan?

- Will there be enough wall space for all those paintings and mementoes?

- Do you want a one or two car garage? A two car garage helps with the resale value.

- Will wash house laundry facilities in the garage be adequate?

- Consider clothes lines and clothes dryers.

- Do you require room for a vegetable garden? Do you want a patio BBQ area? How much lawn do you want to mow?

- Double glazing is now a requirement of most district building codes. Other money and energy saving possibilities include installation of a heat pump, solar water heating and good quality lined drapes.

- What sort of heating will you install? An open fire may look and feel good, but in many towns and cities open fires are prohibited. What about a heat pump? It requires little maintenance and can also act as an air conditioner on hot and humid summer days. Consider an internal ducting system to circulate heat from under the roof throughout the house.

Make sure that whoever designs your house hears your requirements and includes them in the design. You are the one paying out your life savings for your dream home. Get what you want, what you need and what you have dreamt about.

There will be a contract to sign. Read it carefully, every detail, and ask all your questions before you sign. Get your solicitor to check it out. And insist on some indication in the contract of the occupation / completion date. It is now quite common to have a contractual completion date, with penalties for running over time.

Note very carefully what the penalties are if you wish to change any detail of the design during the building process. Changes are costly and may even require the issue of a new council building consent.

And if you do decide to build a new home, make that decision in plenty of time to ensure that you do not have to rent accommodation between homes. Arrange the timing of the sale of one home and the occupation of your new home as close as possible together. This avoids renting and the cost of storing your effects. Rental and storage can be costly.

Well there it is. These are the housing options. No, I am not trying to shift everyone on at age 65. There are many reasons why you should stay living right where you are. Firstly, our houses become our homes. A home is a place where love, experience and memories reside. Secondly, the longer we live in our homes the more we get attached to them. We get emotionally attached to the place where family, friendship and growing up have been experienced and enjoyed. There are significant memories associated with the places where we have lived, and memories are a most important part of our lives. Perhaps Dad built the house, or we say to ourselves, "This is where we came when we were married, it was our first home. Dad carried me across the doorstep, and we have been so happy living here." Do not minimise the wrench it takes to move away from the place in which we invested our lives and the lives of our children. For many of us the answer to the question, "What about housing: where shall we live?" is, "Stay put."

Interests and hobbies

I met Mr Fugier while he was in hospital recovering from a lung infection. We had many discussions. I remember one particular day, he wanted to do all the talking. He told me of his busy working life. He told me of his utter frustration with retirement. His wife had saved up a long list of tasks to do around the house to keep him busy. He also kept a good vegetable garden and spent much of each day in his garden shed smoking. As he talked it became apparent that Mrs Fugier had driven him out of the house with her long list of demands and instructions. I have not forgotten the frustration he expressed when he said, "What do you do when you have fixed all the windows and oiled all the bloody door hinges?"

What do you do when retirement measures up to less than your expectations? After years of going off to work each day, it can be somewhat daunting to find that you are getting under your wife's feet and she under yours. Perhaps one solution is to turn the garden shed into your personal retreat.

There are two concerns here. Firstly, you do need your own space, your personal time and your own interests. If you have not developed your own hobbies and activities throughout your married life, you are in big trouble when you retire and realise that you are with your partner all day every day for the rest of your life. Take hold of your individuality and find ways to express it. Come to grips with the need for each of you to have your own interests. Give each other the space to feel fulfilled. There will be some parts of your life that your partner is not interested in sharing. That is OK. Give each other space to do your own thing and enrich each other by sharing the pleasure gained from your interest when you are together.

Secondly, with retirement there could well be new interests that you would like to pursue. Some of these you may choose to share. Play bridge, join a petanque club, take up marquetry, go trout fishing or find a local book club. And remember, you are not required to do everything with your partner just because you are retired. Enrol for a post-graduate course, take up wood carving, learn how to make cheese, join the local native bush restoration volunteers — there are a thousand activities that you have not previously had time to pursue. Do some new activity together and also take up some new interests that will enrich you as an individual.

Soon after I retired, I was mowing the grass edge in our street when an older woman returning from her afternoon bridge club stopped to chat. "I suppose you've joined all the local clubs?" she asked. Frankly I didn't know what she was talking about. Now I have discovered that there are a lots of clubs and interests for senior people. The RSA provides good food and drinking companions. Probus stretches the mind and provides an introduction to new interests and new friends.

Churches have a range of programmes for seniors, some for men, most for women — fitness, craft, caring for others, running food banks and Sunday worship. Church activities usually centre on Sunday. There are many friendship groups run by churches that offer time together and good conversation. They also encourage people of all ages to think seriously about the deeper values of life and to share each Sunday in shaping these values into meaningful worship.

Service clubs continue to meet specific community and social needs. They are often involved in projects that provide community facilities, or assistance that meets particular community needs.

How about joining Senior Net? This organisation offers training in basic computer skills and programmes, which you may use for writing, accounting, communication, filing your photographs, accessing family tree history and much more.

U3A, University of the Third Age, offers stimulating speakers and information about current scientific, social and political directions.

Charities are always looking for volunteers. Grey Power and other seniors groups keep the interests of seniors before the public and the Government.

Perhaps you enjoy the cut and thrust of good debate. Political parties are good at creating think tanks and making submissions regarding community and social interests. Or you may decide to deliver party pamphlets to letterboxes and at the same time get some needed exercise.

Those who have been physically active most of their lives will want to continue their sports and fitness activities. Enrol at a gym. Join a walking group. Go to the swim centre several times a week. There is no doubt that those who exercise regularly live healthy and long lives. If your body won't stand the physical activity, but you still want to continue your sporting interest, offer to become involved in club administration. Today's health and fitness industry is in a boom phase, driven by seniors who want to stay fit for living.

One of the great retirement dreams is to travel. Rona from our local church decided to tour with a party to Thailand. When she returned home I asked her how she had enjoyed the trip, and if she had met and talked with many Thai people. She replied, "No, they were all Australians in our bus, and we had to go to MacDonald's because the food was all Chinese." When asked if she had bought home any souvenirs, Rona replied, "Just a pair of snake skin shoes." I thought travel was about meeting other people, sharing their cultures and eating their food. Travel is enriched if you learn a few words of greeting, share a few new ideas and grow a little in the process. Travel is about expanding your own world and mindset.

Don't forget the cost of your chosen hobby or sport. Will your income be able to support your dream to sail the Pacific? Choose an activity that is within your financial grasp. Hobbies can be expensive.

Perhaps I'm too idealistic, or naive, but retirement offers the opportunity to let your mind travel. Our first trip to a non-European cultural country was to Indonesia, to Bali. My sister said to me before we travelled, "The journey is not about where you go, but about the experience and the people and the ideas that you meet along the way." That could also be true for many other aspects of life as a senior.

The joy of being a grandparent

Someone very wise once said, "It's great being a grandparent. You get to pick and choose, to say 'yes' and to say 'no.' You get the chance to do again all those things that you remember enjoying from your childhood. You can make darts and fly kites. You can swing on the long rope out over the river again. And when the day is over and their mother has just left to take them all home, you get to just sit."

It is a real joy being a grandparent, but remember, your grandchildren will always have more energy than you. They will run, dance and play football or cricket for hours, while all you can do is sit and watch, give a few hugs, clap and rejoice at a home run, and occasionally wipe away a few of their tears.

There are grandparents who live half a world away from their families, for whom it takes a supreme saving effort and 24 exhausting hours, enduring a plane flight, before you even see them. And then it's all hugs and greetings and all you want to do is catch some sleep. And it's all over in a flood of departure tears two weeks later when you head home.

Then there are those whose grandchildren live next door. We are onsite when the cricket ball comes over the fence and occasionally smashes a window. We are there to mow lawns and keep their garden. The phone goes and we find ourselves baby sitting again. The grand-kids have given up going to their Dad to get toys repaired and come straight to Gran-pa.

It actually is a privilege to be loved and sought out and to be able to help. Age, energy levels and distance constraints shape and dictate the sort of grandparenting that is possible. It will be different for everyone.

It's time to sound another warning. While it is most enjoyable and a privilege to be a loved grandparent, don't let that privilege become an assumed duty. It's called the baby sitter trap. It is all to easy for working parent families to assume that Gran and Pa will collect the kids from school, take them to their sports, help with their paper run, hang the washing out, take the washing in, peel the spuds and prepare an evening meal. Taking on such commitments will not help you to follow your dreams.

Most of us when we retire have a long wish list of activities for our senior years, things we haven't had time for alongside busy working lives. There is a big difference between being an extra pair of hands and being a grandparent.

There are some qualities that should always be part of the experience. Being a grandparent means that you have a responsibility to share the family story. How did you meet grandma/grandpa? Where did your parents come from before they migrated here? Tell them about camping out in the bush every summer and living off fish and shellfish. Share the stories behind the treasured pieces of silver in Grandma's china cabinet. Tell them about the uncle who went off to the war and came home with a shed full of radio communication equipment. They need to know that their Great-grandad on their mother's side was alcoholic and, in a drunken state, burnt down his bakery business. Tell of the travel you have done and the people you have met. Your grandchildren will be interested that when you were a child you met the Prime Minister, Sir Walter Nash. Whatever you do and whatever you have done, tell the story. It will convey the values that grandchildren are important members of an exciting family and that they too can become important within their community. And let them glean from the stories a sense of what is right and wrong, of what has meaning and what is truly important. In sharing the story of the family you also share the values of the family.

It's not always about talk. Listen to your grandchildren. They often know more than we do. If we listen carefully we will learn about life as it surges around us, and we will be able to use that knowledge and experience. When we moved into our new home the phones needed installing. Our ten year old grandson, who wanted to know how he could help, offered to set up the phones. I really did not know how to do that task. To my surprise he completed the job in about 20 minutes and wanted to know what else needed doing.

Take an interest in and be prepared to discuss what grandchildren are doing at school. Don't be surprised if at age ten they are doing work you did at high school. Grandchildren know about prehistoric reptiles and super novas. These pieces of science were not part of our education. We were just beginning to understand continental drift. Our grandchildren are now learning about molecular converters, the Cern super collider and god particles. Listen to your grandchildren and you too will learn.

Modern grandparenting is not about rules and disciplines and trying to preserve what was important from your own childhood. I was not allowed to clean my motorbike on Sunday. We were not allowed to shop on Sunday. I once suffered punishment because I suggested that Mum buy a cabbage on Sunday. Someone had forgotten to do so on Saturday. We went without cabbage that day. Times and morality have changed. As a child we rode our bikes everywhere. With increased road traffic that can now be quite dangerous. I was required to wear a tie and a school cap to secondary school. I just can't imagine similar requirements and values today. Remember your childhood and pass on your experience of being a child. But also remember that you cannot relive the early years of last century. Neither does the post-scientific, electronic communication generation want to relive those years.

Being a grandparent is not about trying to preserve a way of life that is always passing away. Much as we might like to pass on the rules and disciplines of our childhood, living in today's world is not about reliving the experiences of the past. Life and culture have moved on. We live no longer in the age of hard manual work. We live in the information sharing age that depends upon good fast communication.

Put it this way, when we were at primary school, most of us in the 60 up generation were taught facts using the rote learning technique. We were not taught to ask questions, but just the opposite; we were taught to accept without question the facts that the teacher and the standard curriculum determined we would require in life. Today's children are encouraged to ask questions. The teacher's task is both to understand the questions and to point to where the answers can be found. Teaching is no longer about the teacher giving answers; it is about children finding answers. That is quite different. If as grandparents we try to provide all the answers we are in danger of trying to repeat the ways and mistakes of previous generations.

To share wisdom with the next generation is one of the greatest gifts that a grandparent can give to a child. Make sure that that you share wisdom and insight for a new generation, not the facts and morality of a past generation.

And finally, let your grandchildren be your teacher. One way to keep up with all the changes that infiltrate our fast changing world is through children. It is their world and they must live in it. One of the best ways of staying young at heart is to see the world through the eyes of a child. Jesus said, "Except you become as little children, you will not enjoy the kingdom." Such wise words require us not only to value the lives of children, but to learn from them and with them. It is a privilege to enter their world of thinking and growing, expressing and sharing their enthusiasm for life. We achieve this every time we allow a child to become our teacher.

Finance and money matters

"It has been a hard road for Colin Anderson over the past few months. Every day the 65 year old has climbed on his bike and cycled a 65km lap of Lake Taupo. Yesterday he completed his 65th lap, one for each year of his life. He spent seven to eight hours each day in the saddle, getting only about four hours rest each night. And he has not quite finished. On Sunday he will hop on his bike once more to ride a final lap, this time with his wife and 30 mates. He set off in February 2013 on this quest and has raised $5,000 for the child cancer organisation Canteen. He has clocked up 19,400km in 53 days riding."

Mike Watson, Fairfax NZ News, 20 April 2013.

In our world money matters. Even a pleasure ride to celebrate the 65th milestone can become an opportunity to raise funds for a charitable cause. Occasionally we are able to persuade ourselves that other interests, neighbourliness, fitness, community spirit and love are what really matter. Yes they do, but always lurking in the background is the need to pay for everything. Money really matters. If you want to have adequate real life choices, money certainly matters. To fail to plan ahead so that there are funds in the bank, spells a retirement of strict budgeting, keeping a watching eye on every dollar and cent, and being dependent on NZ Superannuation. That shape for life makes it almost impossible to travel, even to the South Island, and impossible to update your car every five years. It means that regular café breaks, ice creams and cream donuts may not be on the menu. (Cream donuts should be out anyway; the cholesterol count is far too high.) If you haven't saved a considerable nest egg for the day you retire you are doomed to a bare necessities lifestyle. The message is, start saving when you start work. Most of us didn't hear that at the time; so the message now is, start saving when you are 50. And if you didn't hear that message either, budget very carefully for a no frills retirement.

How much do I need to save for my retirement? There are so many unknowns and people's tastes and choices vary so much, that it's a bit like asking, "How long is a piece of string?" However, budget advisors and banking gurus suggest that we should have saved around $400,000, if we want to have a comfortable old age. The plain fact of the matter is that most of us haven't. Most of us begin retirement from a less than comfortable financial position. There are however, some guidelines that make sound common sense.

We will deal with the big ticket items first:

• Start saving as soon as you can. It is never too early to get a retirement nest egg together.

• By the time you retire, own your own home freehold. Do not have a mortgage to pay off.

• Make sure that you have a late model reliable car that will have a good resale value. Change it every five years until you no longer need a car. This will keep your vehicle relatively maintenance free, and with regular services you will keep running costs low. Choose a car that suits your needs. You may have regular trips with grandchildren and all their gear. Don't even look at low swept sports models. You will soon get tired of sitting almost prone and having to lever yourself out of the seats. Remember that with aging, bones grow old and muscles get tired.

• As you near retirement begin to replace your household appliances. The last thing you want is to come home from a two week break to find that your freezer has passed away and that you have quantities of food oozing out across the kitchen floor to meet you. Make sure that when you retire your washing machine, freezer, fridge, telephones, computer, heaters and other appliances are in new, or almost new, condition. (Small appliances, including tools you may need if you intend to have a workshop, are relatively cheap to replace or purchase later.)

• Try to pay cash for everything you purchase. And because you are paying cash, ask for a discount. This saves considerable amounts on interest payments. Why should the lending company have your hard earned cash? And while you are at it, get air points and Fly Buys points that will give you a bonus free trip to Australia or the Pacific every so often. If you decide to build a house for your retirement, the air points earned will get you a considerable way round the world.

• Shop around. Try to buy on special. Junk mail in your letterbox can be a real pain, but read it if you want to know what deals and discounts are on offer. Prices do vary from place to place.

Small ticket items, the necessities for each day, like bread, milk, most groceries and vegetables, are a different matter. You often need them at that moment. Even clothing comes into the small ticket category. Because it is so easy to spend on small and low cost items, it is even more important to have a budget. It has to be a significant saving before you buy in bulk or are tempted to spend above your grocery or clothing budget.

- Buy carefully. Is it what you really want?

- Compare prices of competing brands. Read your junk mail.

- While you are checking the labels, check out the fat content and the sugar content. Is it healthy food? Has the food been over-processed. Does it contain high levels of preservative and colour additives?

- Where is the article processed and packaged? Do you wish to support local industry?

- Consider the cost of big brands compared to plain label and proprietary brands. These are not always more reasonably priced.

- Be careful with bulk buy deals. Often, small weight items on special are more expensive than buying larger quantities. Sometimes the small quantity on special can be more economical.

- Have a list of what you need to buy. Keep to the list and avoid the random shopping tendency to buy what you see. Shop shelving and displays are very cleverly designed to catch the attention of random shoppers and browsers. Even coloured packaging is designed to attract your attention. Shop only when you know what you want.

- Often articles with lower mark ups are high up or low down on shelves. Sometimes items reduced or on special are at the back of shops, particularly in clothing outlets.

- Dashing around several outlets, in the hope of finding a bargain, may result in spending more on petrol than you save on the goods.

- Join loyalty schemes so that you get the loyal customers' discounts and specials

- Weekly saving for Christmas. The most expensive month of the year is December. Gifts and food all add to the celebration but overheat the monthly budget. You could join the supermarket Christmas club. But don't join one of the Christmas food parcel schemes, as they give you little choice of food parcel contents and are expensive. Alternatively, run your own Christmas savings scheme by having a monthly savings budget specifically earmarked to be spent in December. That way you pay no fees and you get the interest. Manage your own Christmas costs and be sure to watch out for those pre-Christmas specials.

There are many other ways of managing your weekly shopping costs. Check out the bulk bin shops. Washing powder is much cheaper in bulk. There are bulk meat buying schemes, but for this you will need a freezer. Explore the many uses of washing soda, that much-used cleanser from grandma's day. Use your freezer to store fruit and vegetables purchased more cheaply in season.

Do you really need to buy a newspaper? Many newspaper articles can be accessed for free on the Internet. You can read any newspaper from any country in the world. Why pay for one to be delivered? And if you have a smartphone you can even read the Internet news wherever you are.

While on smartphones, you don't need to annually purchase a diary — use the one appended to the calendar appointment programme on your phone. Also you can use the Memo pad as a shopping reminder list. Cross off each article as you put it in the shopping trolley. Somewhere in that very smart gadget you will also find the weather report, an alarm clock, a programme to share photos of the grandchildren, a camera, an FM radio and a calculator. There are a multitude of apps (Applications) that you can install to allow your smartphone to do what you want it to do. Ask at the cell phone shops about what is possible. But be prepared to pay a little extra for a smartphone that will do wonderful things.

One very clever application is the GPS Navigator programme. Tell your smartphone where you want to go, follow its spoken instructions and see its directions on the screen. You will arrive at your destination, with no detours and no paper maps to fight with in the limited front seat space of your car. The GPS app on your phone will get you there following the shortest route. Alternatively, for about $150 you can purchase a dedicated GPS unit with free map updates. They usually come with Australian and

New Zealand maps. For an additional cost you can buy maps for any other country. The initial outlay costs are quickly recouped in petrol savings. A GPS will also stop all those front seat arguments about whether to turn left or right.

Do check out your taxation entitlement once you retire. With a reduced income you could well be in a different tax bracket and thus need to pay less tax. Consequently there could be a considerable tax refund waiting for you. Make sure that you are paying income tax at the correct rate. Also put in a tax refund application claiming any tax returns owed. It may pay for a few days in Australia.

We live in a world where prices always seem to be rising, over which you have no control. If you don't pay you don't get the service. But you can review the costs annually, or when the company reworks its costs and passes increases on to you, the consumer. The power account is one of these. Shop around power companies to find the best deal for you. Likewise your household insurance cover, telephone services, pay television services, even the doctor and medical services — shop around. A word of caution. With doctors you are dealing with someone who knows you and your long term health needs. It may be wise to stay with the one you know and pay the extra. Join all the membership and discount schemes that you can. Retailer's loyalty card schemes are a way for them to get to know their customers' needs. Make no mistake about it they are in business to make money. But there are significant cash backs, discounts and birthday presents for card holders. Joining up can be worth your while.

There is one area of budgeting to which we give little thought, the cost of a funeral. We are all going to die and someone has to meet the funeral costs. And remember if you are married there will be two accounts from the funeral director. Start putting that money aside. There are insurance policies that can help. If you die on the job, the circumstances may determine that your employer meets the funeral costs from their insurance cover on their workers. There will also be incidental costs: flowers, some catering, family to be accommodated and extra running of the family car. Your family may gather round to help with these, but be prepared to meet small costs that will all mount up.

And don't forget that if your spouse dies first, when the funeral is over there is the hassle of reworking your budget. Your income will be halved if you depend on National Superannuation, but your expenses will not. You will only have one Superanuation payment providing income, but many of the costs of running your home will remain the same. It is likely that only food, clothing, personal items and medical expenses will be halved. Insurance cover, rates, running the car, the telephone and power bills, are substantial costs that will show little change.

Perhaps you are hoping that a rich uncle will remember you on his death bed. It does happen, but don't plan on it happening. Your budget should only include what you know your income will be. On the expense side you may decide to be more generous. Setting aside funds for what might happen can be seen as a specific ear-marked saving. This is what we all do if we decide to save for a large ticket item some time in the future.

I have emphasised the need to plan and save. That is only half the equation. The other half is to spend wisely all you can so that you can enjoy your senior years. It is counter-productive to go without so that your family will eventually have a good inheritance. They probably earn more than you ever earned. Save so that you can spend to enjoy your life long dreams.

On the next page is a sample budget. It is included as a model showing the categories which you may want to include in your budget. It is not intended that you should adopt this budget as your own. You will have different interests and priorities that must be built into your budget.

Sample Monthly Budget

January 2013	
Monthly Income	
NZ Superannuation 1	$1,073
NZ Superannuation 2	$1,073
Employer's Pension	$418
Total Monthly income	**$2,564**
Annual Expenses	
(Set aside monthly to accumulate until required)	
Insurance Car	$97
Insurance Household	$140
Car repairs and running	$50
Council Rates	$175
Water Rates	$155
Holidays	$100
Health: Doctor Chemist Dentist	$130
Power	$150
LPG Gas	$40
Christmas	$70
Birthdays	$40
Deposited in an interest bearing account	**$1,147**
Monthly Expenses	
Groceries, fruit and vegetables	$860
Petrol	$150
Telecom	$99
Mobile phone	$46
Savings account	$262
Banked monthly to operate a Credit Card	**$1,417**
Total expenses per month	**$2,564**

Note that this budget does not go into fine detail for a range of expenses. It allows for a certain amount of flexibility in personal spending on clothes, toiletries, etc. Similarly, gardening costs (usually for the vegetable garden), café costs, club fees and magazine subscriptions. If your home is almost new and built of low maintenance materials, you may decide that there is, as yet, no need to budget for repair and maintenance costs.

This budget does not allow for equipment repairs, maintenance of property and incidental expenses. These items must be paid out of savings. If your household appliances are aging it would be wise to budget for repairs and replacements.

The category 'Groceries, Fruit and Vegetables' includes café stops and occasionally dining out.

Extra holiday expenses come from savings.

A caution: Unless you feel absolutely confident to operate a budget that only lists general categories, as this example does, it would be wise to have a much more detailed budget.

The use of Internet banking to access your bank accounts has the advantage that you can manage your accounts on a daily basis. You can shift funds from one account to another quickly and easily. Think carefully before you do so, as such action may upset other parts of your budget. It is no use putting extra funds into the Christmas account if it depletes your electricity budget. The power bill must be paid.

If you regularly overspend in one area of your budget, it is obvious that your budget allocation in the area is not adequate. Rework your budget, cutting back in other categories, so that your budget balances. When you have a limited fixed income you cannot regularly overspend.

Note: This is a monthly budget. If you are used to fortnightly income you will want to follow a fortnightly budget.

Being single in a partners world

When my work moved me to Wanganui we were thousands of kilometres from our children's grandparents, our parents. That was when Maggie came into our home and into our lives. Maggie offered to child mind when my wife and I had evening activities to attend. Maggie remembered birthdays and Christmas. She would phone to wish the Children 'Happy Birthday.' And it was Maggie who often arrived with a hot evening meal to share. Maggie had been widowed about five years before we knew her. Since her husband died suddenly while mowing the lawns, she had learned to drive, successfully gained her drivers licence and had become a regular taxi service for many of her senior friends. When Maggie answered the phone she would always say, "It's myself here." Maggie was a true friend.

While most of what I am sharing in this book will be helpful to those approaching retirement, it has been written largely with the assumption that most will be married or have a partner when they reach the 60 plus milestone. For many this will not be your experience. Some will find that in their senior years they are alone, having chosen to remain single, or their partner may have already passed away.

One of today's choices in a culture of equal opportunity is to remain single. Some will choose to promote their career opportunities. Others will find themselves single as the outcome of a painful accident or separation. Singleness was the experience of many in a passing generation whose partners and fiancés went off to serve their country overseas and never returned. Some fell in love with the wrong person, one who was not free to marry, and others just never found quite the right person to love.

Whatever the reason for being a single person facing old age, there will be moments when you ask yourself, why? Why me in a world of partners? There may well be moments of regret and moments of sadness. Let's not dwell on the difficulties of singleness, for there are also positives about being single. The task of single people preparing to retire is to make positive choices that will assist their retirement well-being.

The most obvious difference that must be faced as a single retiree is that there will only be a single retirement income. Unless you have managed to save a significant financial nest egg, very strict budgeting will be essential and every cent will count. It becomes even more important to have a debt-free home, no mortgage or loan repayments, and reliable household appliances. Reliable transport is a must. A car replacement saving in your budget is a sound proposition. You do not want continual maintenance costs on your vehicle, and you do want the savings to be there when the replacement of your car becomes necessary.

While we are talking of car maintenance, make sure that you have a good mechanic. Find a good service centre and take your car to the same person for servicing on each occasion. In this way you will get good advice from someone who knows your vehicle. They will be able to tell you when to keep it and when to replace it.

The same advice goes for other tradespeople. Get to know a reliable plumber, electrician and odd job person. You may want to have someone to mow your lawns and someone to clean your windows. It is a good idea to have the outside walls of your house water blasted once a year to get rid of winter dust and mould.

Like any other retired person it will be a good idea to have someone to whom you can go for financial advice — an accountant or bank advisor. There may be questions that a lawyer needs to address. Get good professional advice on questions relating to property purchase and sale, how to approach neighbours, and how to negotiate with civic authorities regarding your rights and responsibilities as a good neighbour.

If, as a single person, you feel the need to have children and young people in your life there are ways of doing just that. Local schools are always looking for mature people to hear children's reading. The local library may also be looking for suitable volunteer readers for the children's corner. If you want to work with children there may have to be a police character check of your criminal record before you get the job.

In this very modern world grandchildren often live thousands of miles from their grandparents. If you do not have grandchildren, or cannot visit your own grandchildren regularly, get to know the families in your street and community and become a surrogate grandparent to a family whose real grandparents are a world away. You can remember children's birthdays with a small gift. Adopted grandchildren are a lot of fun. There is something very special about holding a small hand in yours.

If you don't want children around, but would like someone to talk to, get a pet. Sally lived by herself but had two King Charles spaniels. It was her delight to talk to them, she would tell you that they answered back. She groomed them, walked them and did everything for them. They did in fact become her children. It is well known that people who keep pets, who each day have to feed clean and exercise them, live longer.

Communities are full of social groups and activities for seniors. Travel clubs, Grey Power, coffee clubs, book reading circles, historical societies and Church activities all offer opportunities to make friends and have fun.

There may be openings in your community to become responsible for a significant community task. Community groups and sports clubs are always looking for secretaries and treasurers. The skills and contacts that you acquired during your working life may be just the input that a community group requires. Doing voluntary community work also has the additional benefit of giving personal worth and meaning to your living. You give some of your time and skill to the community and in return you gain something to live for.

You don't have to be single to travel, but travel is one of the great activities of retired people. It is a way of meeting people and getting a new perspective on cultures and customs that shape the lives of people all over the world. As it is more expensive to travel as a single person, it may assist you to travel with a trusted friend. Be very careful about your choice of travelling companion. If you wish to travel with a companion, try short weekends and weekly trips, before you commit to three months touring Europe together.

The loneliness of having no close family for support and encouragement can be quite a burden. The responsibility of making all the decisions and acting upon them alone can be onerous. It is not easy to live alone, but with careful thought, and a willingness to think and plan ahead, there will be something each day about which you can smile.

Health: Medical matters

In 1998 we lived in the UK. While there, we took a friend to Wales to the village to which he had been evacuated as a child during the London blitz. We enquired around but could find no one that he had known during his stay. But we did have a most enjoyable hour chatting about wartime memories with a small group of elderly women who remembered the war years very clearly. We found them in a café having their weekly coffee together. That day was a good health day for each of us.

One of the most important aspects of becoming a senior is to retain good health. There are those who have not seen a doctor for years, and there are others who seem to be visiting the doctor every few weeks, or even days. It is quite certain that in our senior years we will need the help of health professionals. It is very likely that we will become regular daily pill poppers. It is predictable that our bodies will slow down so that our physical reactions are considerably slower than they were when we were in our prime. Our hearing may be fading and our eyesight may require the help of an optician.

Now before you get too depressed about your prospects, let me add that the anxiety caused by our advanced years and declining health can be considerably relieved if we have regular medical checks. In this way we are helped to become familiar with our aging bodies. There are those who are proud that they have never seen a doctor or that they take no medication. Then there are those who, with the help of their doctor, are aware of their hypertension/high blood pressure, know how to diet, avoid stressful situations and exercise regularly. They know their bodies, are aware of the path their aging may take, and are taking daily steps to minimise the problems they may have to live with. A great deal of worry can be avoided if we are aware of what might happen, and accept the advice and experience of medical professionals.

I really do mean the professional experts. Anecdotal information shared over a cup of tea, or a few drinks, may be as suspect as old wives' tales. Television advertisements for health wonder products, and so called reality interview shows, may have little to do with your particular health needs. On the other hand the good advice of doctors, opticians, dentists and qualified health professionals is worth its weight in gold.

There are a host of minor health matters. I will mention a few that may come your way.

Bending becomes a problem. Putting on socks or stockings may require the help of someone else if you can no longer bend to reach your toes. The same goes for scratching that back itch. Age is often accompanied by a stiffening of joints. The simple act of turning your head to look at something behind may require you to turn your whole body. This becomes quite important when you are waiting at a crossing for traffic to pass. Have a talk with your doctor. You may be in the early stages of arthritis.

As hearing deteriorates it may become quite irksome to always be asking people to repeat what they are saying. The time will come when, if you are having difficulty hearing, you will have to visit an audiologist to get fitted with a hearing aid. That will be quite an expensive exercise. And don't leave it too late as it takes a few months to get used to the increased sound levels that an aid offers. With hearing aids the world sounds very noisy. Every sound, even those we have long since disregarded, is magnified. With perseverance each sound is given a new value and put in its place. I remember the day I got my hearing aids; I could hear the leaves rustling in the trees and my shoe laces slapping on my shoes as I walked. Trucks roared by creating audio havoc and a dropped pair of scissors sounded like a freight train passing. It would have been easy to put the aids back in their box for good during those first months. Area Health Boards have subsidies for those for whom an aid is necessary for their work. It therefore makes sense, if your hearing is failing, to get it checked out before you retire. It may pay to think ahead.

Aging may bring with it deterioration in our vision. As we read we may find ourselves holding the newspaper further away. Phone book names and numbers may become blurred. It's time to see an optician.

A word about being too health conscious. There are those who with every ache and pain run to the doctor, reach for their health books or launch their Internet browser to diagnose their latest itch. We imagine every pain and scratch to be some serious malady. As we age we do get aches and pains. There will be days when we feel off colour, when we just want to rest and read a good book.

At age 60 and over you can't expect to have the energy that you had at 40. It probably isn't possible any longer to sprint faster than your teenaged grandson. At 60 it's time to sit back and enjoy the energy that the younger generation is so keen to demonstrate.

There are some free health measures that are a must do. Get that pre-winter influenza jab. Vaccination against flu is a must if you want to actively enjoy the winter months. It is free. Just ask for the vaccination each April when you are at the clinic.

The other free service that comes to mind is to get an annual check for sugar levels. Diabetes is becoming a major illness worldwide. Get blood tests done. If you do have this ailment it can be treated with a few changes to your diet, or in serious cases, with daily injections. This treatment is comprehensive and free. It offers you an opportunity to adjust your diet, establish a helpful exercise programme and become more aware of your body's daily needs.

Keeping good health is all about knowing your own health needs, and taking the correct steps to keep your body, mind and spirit in tune.

Health and doctor's visits

See your doctor on a regular basis. By the time we retire most of us will be doing just that for some complaint or other. At least once a year get your doctor to give you a full check up. We are all a bit frightened by cancer. Diagnose it early and you have a much better chance of survival. High blood pressure or 'hypertension' can lead to all sorts of heart/cardiac complications. Get it checked out annually.

Don't hesitate to ask questions about your health. It's your body so get the answers you deserve. Share with your doctor any small incidents that you think may be significant. You felt dizzy. You have tripped up a couple of times lately. You always seem to have a cough or a cold. It's not complaining unnecessarily, and it's certainly not putting the doctor to any trouble. Tell the doctor you are puffing when you get to the top of the stairs. That is exactly what I shared with my doctor and a fortnight later I was having a heart bypass operation. It's your life and your body, and what you have observed may well be significant to your good healthy future. So get to know your doctor. Treat him/her as a friend who is really interested in you. Ask all the questions you have and make sure that you get answers that you understand. Medicine is no longer the mysterious world of a few. Medical information is on the Internet for everyone to read. If you don't understand all the doctor has told you, look it up. Knowing about your health and your body has long term benefits.

Health issues can sometimes generate a crisis. Crisis alarms are available from St John's for a small charge. It is also wise to become a St John's member if you have no transport available. You may need an ambulance in a health crisis.

Balancing Diet, Weight and Physical Fitness

We live in a culture that is weight conscious. Consequently, when we think of diet we associate it with weight. Our bathrooms are incomplete if they do not have a set of scales. Consciously we associate low weight with good health. Diet, weight, exercise, our character, our spirituality and our interests are all linked together in the good health package. It's best not to isolate each of these but to see them as a complete package, each component adding to the balance of the others. Our BMI (Body Mass Indicator) reading is only able to measure our height and weight. It tells us nothing about our character, attitudes or ambitions. All these, and all sorts of other facets of our lives, contribute to our overall good health and fitness.

Low Fat Diet

There are guidelines that can and should be followed. Most of us will benefit from a low sugar, low fat diet. The emphasis has for some years, been on a low fat diet. Takeaway foods are taking a hammering, as are convenience and prepared supermarket foods. The emphasis should be on knowing what you are eating. As far as possible prepare your own meals. Then you will know what's in them. Cut excessive fat off meat. Grill sausages and chicken so that the fat drains away. Get a George Foreman Grill or similar. It is designed to drain fat off as it grills. Cheese is almost entirely fat. The aim should be not to deprive yourself of fatty food, but to consume fat in manageable amounts that your body can process. So eat cheese sparingly. Reduced fat milk is bearable. A soy bean product *So Good* really is a delicious non-fat milk substitute. Use canola oil or olive oil for frying instead of fat or butter. Have only one piece of toast each morning with just a smear of butter, not melted and running everywhere. Better still, use a vegetable oil based spread. Look up cardiac dietary information to get good tips on low fat diets. There is plenty of information in the bookshops and on the Internet.

Low sugar diets

These are a different story. New Zealand is near the top of the list of countries with a diabetic problem. We are consuming far too much sugar and our bodies are not producing enough insulin to balance the increased sugar levels. The message is: consume less sugar and do more exercise to burn off the energy that sugar provides. Here are some practical sugar reduction ideas. If you must have sweet tasting food there are sugar substitutes available in supermarkets. Read the food label and choose food and drink with low sugar content. Eat fruit. Stop adding sugar to coffee and tea. Do we really need all that potato and starchy food? Starch converts to sugar and fat in the body. Eat more green vegetables. Cut out all soft drinks and have freshly squeezed fruit juice instead. After a couple of months on a low sugar diet, foods with significant amounts of sugar taste far too sweet to enjoy.

It seems that our bodies have adjusted to enjoy high fat, high sugar diets. This partly comes about because we are not doing as much exercise as we used to; we no longer burn off these high energy foods with exercise. Hence it's a balancing act as excess sugar is converted to fat which is stored in our bodies. The secret is to balance our consumption with exercise, so that we consume energy at the same rate at which we expend energy.

Physical Fitness

The experts and fitness fanatics all tell us that we need to exercise not less than 30 minutes a day, five days a week, so that our bodies sweat. Walking, bike riding, jogging, bowling, fishing, riding an exercise cycle, swimming and going to the gym are popular ways to keep fit. The important thing is to get started and to plan your daily life so that it includes exercise. It is not an optional extra. There are some daily and weekly tasks that count as exercise: mowing the lawn, digging the garden, dusting and vacuuming the house and hanging out the washing.

Many parks now include exercise machines as part of the walkway system. Make use of them as they are much cheaper than going to the gym. Join an aerobics class or a swim session. If you are exerted to the point of getting up a sweat then it counts as exercise. A warning note: choose the right exercise regime for you. One of the failings for many elderly people is that it's pretty easy to break a bone. As we age our bones become chalky, especially those of women. Drink milk and eat vegetables to increase your calcium intake. If you dislike milk have a talk with your doctor about calcium supplements. Whatever you choose it should be a pleasure, not an imposition.

A health insurance policy cover may have assisted you to get prompt medical and surgical attention. In retirement this may become one of the cuts that will assist you to live within your more limited budget. Before you cancel the policy, be aware that any specialist care you require may, in the public health system, be delayed for months while you wait for an appointment. Think about the repercussions very carefully before you cancel the policy.

Men who feel they need regular exercise can try the local boxing gym, the swimming pool, walking, digging the neighbour's garden or mowing someone's lawns. Put away the garden blower and sweep the paths instead. Hang the washing out or do the vacuuming for your wife. She may be pleased enough to make you some cheese scones and a good cup of coffee.

There are some activities which hinder health and fitness. Smoking is one of them. It is a complete 'no no.' The residues that smoke leaves in your lungs are a major cause of respiratory illness. A number of the substances deposited in your lungs are carcinogenic and a major cause of lung cancer. Give it up. Another reason to stop smoking is that it is costly. Being a non-smoker will help you manage your budget.

Excessive drinking of alcohol

It's important to have a good, clear and agile mind. Alcohol is a sedative. Drinking makes you feel drowsy. It slows down our reactions. Too much alcohol can cause brain damage. It is also expensive and can play havoc with your carefully calculated budget. On the other hand, my doctor told me on one occasion that a drink a day reduces cholesterol levels. That's good news for those who enjoy a beer after mowing the lawns. It's up to you to know how much to drink and how much to take these comments to heart.

Conversation

Avoid the head in the newspaper syndrome. (These days it's head in smartphone syndrome.) They both kill conversation. Talk with your partner. Get to know your neighbour. Ask them over Saturday afternoon for a drink. Talk with people on the bus. Take a ride on a bus at eight in the morning when workers are making their way to their office towers. Try making conversation with row after row of passengers, all with earphones in their ears and the latest iPhone belting out the hit tunes, the weather and the news. They sit hard up against other passengers crowded into cramped seats, not a word of conversation passing between them. There are always exceptions. On one bus service in Auckland they sing songs on the way to work. The local café is a good place to meet for a chat with a group of friends. Get together with your old school friends for lunch. Observe family anniversaries and birthdays. Invent reasons for a gathering: pension day, last day of the month, have a colour red day, shortest day of the year or Father Christmas's birthday.

Forgetfulness

This is one of the standing jokes about older people. It's true, it happens, and it will happen to you. Where are my car keys? Have you seen my glasses? It's not really a laughing matter. I misplaced the house keys yesterday and I haven't found them yet. No doubt I will come across them in some unusual place; or maybe even somewhere very obvious. It is a source of annoyance. (After note: The keys have been located, perfectly clean, in the pocket of a pair of shorts that had been through the washing machine.) It's not only car keys. It's people's names, phone numbers and

45

that pressing task that was a must do next morning. The real frustration is that five minutes after you have said to yourself, "Well what does in matter anyway?" you remember, and by that time you have begun the next task on the list. It seems that this little frustration often accompanies old age. So don't get worried because you are not going crazy. And you certainly are not on your way to full blown Alzheimer's disease. If you can remember that you have forgotten, then you don't have Alzheimer's. It's when you can't remember what you have forgotten, and carry blithely on, that you are in trouble. Friends and family, those who love you and care about you, will love you enough to let you know if this happens.

There is a little test that you can do to find out if someone you care about may be suffering from Alzheimer's. When I began working in an older people's ward the Charge Nurse explained it to me this way. One of the patients, John, was passing by. The nurse threw a piece of paper on the floor and called out, "John, please pick that paper up and put it in the waste basket." John picked up the paper, but could not remember what to do with it next. The second instruction escaped him. That's Alzheimer's. Don't assume too much until you have been to a doctor, had it checked out and been referred on to a specialist, done the tests and had a full diagnosis. It is a difficult disease to diagnose accurately and there are a range of related diseases. Addards, the Alzheimer's Society, is a good source of mental health information.

Forgetfulness can be managed by adopting a range of helpful measures. Write things down. Use a telephone directory, don't try to memorise numbers. Get a mobile phone with a range of good applications, (the jargon is 'apps'), that tell you everything — a memo programme, a note pad, newspaper cuttings, Wikipedia, (that Internet site which is an encyclopaedia of factual information), your grocery shopping list, a calendar and a diary with an alarm reminder — to name a few. These are all available on a good smartphone. You can even create a memo that tells you your own phone number. After all who remembers their cell phone number?

Caution: Create a password on your phone so that only you can access your personal information.

Hospitalisation

The chances are that as you age you will require hospital care. There is an inbuilt, unwarranted anxiety about hospitals. They used to be the place where people went to die, it was a genuine fear. This is no longer the case. Hospitals are in the business of medical and surgical treatment. They exist to help people regain their health. It is a great joy to hospital staff to send people home again fit and well. Today less than 1% of patients die while in hospital care.

When your turn to experience hospital care comes make sure that you make full use of the specialists', doctors' and nursing staff's care. Ask your questions and get answers. Answer their questions fully and truthfully and when the time for your discharge comes, take the advice given, follow the treatment regime offered and take the tablets.

Your time in hospital can be a time for re-evaluation of your lifestyle and re-assessing your personal values. Make the most of the opportunity.

Security and safety

A centenarian who fought back, told of a woman posing as a long-lost relative who stole money using his EFTPOS card. According to his daughter, "The twilight years can be hell for the elderly. Dad was targeted because he lived alone and was kind, trusting and loved company."

"People who target the elderly deliberately are basically greedy scumbags who have lost all form of human decency."

Elder abuse is a single or repeated act, or lack of appropriate action, occurring within any relationship where there is an expectation of trust, which causes harm or distress to an older person.

Anna Leask, NZ Herald, 27 June 2013.

Elder abuse — those who work with the elderly will tell you that there is plenty of it. And it's not the only danger that people in their senior years face. Nurses, doctors, social workers and home help workers tell of older people whose families do not visit, whose only contact with the outside world is the meals on wheels delivery person and the weekly grocery delivery worker. The diminished world of many older people can be a source of danger. We all wish to live in a secure and safe world. Older people need that same security.

There are many ways in which we can take action to make our world more secure. Have outside security doors installed so that you are able to talk with unsolicited visitors through the safety of the screen door.

Tradespeople seeking work by making house calls door-to-door can pressure you into making on the spot decisions. Always ask for some written paperwork outlining the proposed job or service and the cost. Indicate that you will consider their offer and phone back if you require their help. Do not make doorstep decisions. Give yourself time to think it through. Talk about your plans with your family before you decide to spend a large sum of money. Before you agree to any work on your property ask to see the tradesperson's qualification or registration card. Make sure that you get a quality job.

Never let another person handle your credit cards, and never give your PIN (Personal Identification Number) to anyone. Do not write down your PIN. If your credit cards are stolen, phone your bank immediately to request new cards and the can ation of your stolen cards. Do not disclose your financial identification, your PIN. Your PIN is your financial security.

As you age there will be many people who for good reason will come into your home. Friends will always be welcome. The doctor, the health nurse, home care workers, the meals on wheels staff and a host of others will, for good reasons, also cross your doorstep. They will bring you friendship and a little of the outside world as well. Be cautious of those who come unexpectedly, without good reason and who cannot produce identification to support why they have come. Try to encourage those organisations and business that come to your home to always send the same person. They will become friends. They will become your window through which to view the world.

Aging people, especially those who live alone, would be wise to obtain a medical alarm. St John's (freephone 0800 16 16 10) supply these and offer a very efficient ambulance and emergency service. (*See previous chapter*) There will be a cost.

Prescribed medication can be risky if your memory is failing. "Have I already taken my morning tablets or not?" Don't take a second dose until you are sure that you have forgotten the first. For a small charge, you can have the chemist blister pack your tablets, so that a quick look tells you when you have not taken your dose. While on medication, make sure that you get your free flu vaccine injection each winter from your doctor, or your medical centre nurse. One small jab is much better than two or three weeks of painful misery.

There may come a time when you need the support of a walking stick or walking frame. These prevent painful and avoidable falls which may result in broken bones and lead to hospitalisation. If you have had several falls it may be time to get a walking frame. If you do need a walking frame, get one with a seat to rest on while you do the dishes and peel the potatoes. And make sure that it has a basket. It is very awkward, almost impossible, to manoeuvre a frame and carry an object. A comment on personal pride

— sometimes we have to put our personal pride aside and just get on with living. Acquiring a walking frame is, for many seniors, one of those moments.

As we age we don't want to be climbing steps and stairs. Rearrange the house so that all the articles you want to use regularly, and all daily activities, are downstairs, or if you live in a high-rise, on the same level. Rearrange your storage cupboards so that what you need is within reach. You do not want to be climbing a ladder or up on a stool when your legs are a bit wobbly. Get hand grab rails installed in the toilet and the bathroom. Give up stepping into and out of a bath. Instead, use a plastic stool to sit on while showering. Get a cordless phone and take it with you from room to room so that you do not have to dash to the phone. Don't forget to recharge its batteries overnight.

And last but not least, keep your home warm. There is nothing worse for aging people than a cold damp home. Good heaters are very efficient. It will cost a little extra for electricity, but you will be saving if you do not have to visit the doctor regularly. A small tip if you want to keep warm; wear a warm woollen knitted hat. A huge amount of our body heat is lost through our head. And that's not an old wives' tale, it works.

Everyone is going to die

Some years ago Mary died. I met with Jack, her husband, and their family to arrange the funeral service, indicating to them that as I had not met Mary they would have to tell me about her life. They seemed most reluctant to share anything beyond, "She was a good cook and kept a good house." After the funeral service, over a cup of tea, I got talking with Mary's brother. "You handled that muddle well," he said. To my surprise he went on to tell me about the Mary whom the whole street knew, how she would stand at the front gate waiting for Jack to come home, shouting at him as he turned the corner. The whole street heard her rebuking him if he had forgotten to stop at the butcher shop to pick up the sausages for dinner.

When my younger brother died at age 65, he had been receiving National Superannuation for just three days. I found myself considering my own mortality more seriously. I have also become aware that I am now attending more funerals: my friends are dying. The corollary is that one day the funeral I attend will be mine.

One of the few certainties in life is that we will one day die. Most of our life is spent not taking the finality of life very seriously. For many, the religious beliefs they hold will be of considerable help when it comes to both understanding this fact of life and preparing for the experience of death. Without getting too morbid, there are some common sense actions you can take to make the experience of your passing easier for yourself and your family.

Share what you believe about death and dying with your partner and family. Let them know what you want to happen with your remains. Let them know what you want to happen to all your belongings. Most of us have preferences. We may want a religious funeral. We would like music at the farewell celebration, music that we appreciated during our life time. We know who we want to speak so that our life is celebrated. We may prefer just a simple thanksgiving for good years of quality living.

There may be people who we do not want to speak at our funeral. There are usually life experiences that we would rather have forgotten.

Will we be satisfied with a plain wooden casket, or do we want highly polished wood veneer? Who would we wish to read, to sing, to be pallbearers, to participate? There are a host of choices that can be decided quite easily prior to our death if we have talked about our wishes with our family. Get it sorted before you die. Make arrangements ahead of time to meet funeral costs. The cost of a funeral, if not saved for and set aside, can be quite a burden. Those who have belonged to a lodge or Returned Service's Association, will want these groups to be involved in their funeral service. These organisations may also hold funds set aside to help families meet funeral expenses. Talk with your family regarding your wishes. Share with them any arrangements you may have made. Also talk with your parish minister or priest, if you have one, so that your preferences are known regarding the shape and order of the religious service. Alternatively, arrange with a celebrant to conduct your funeral.

One caution, the funeral service is not just about you and your life. It is also about asking God to bless those whom you have loved and with whom you shared life. The funeral service is also for those who are family, who have loved you and who must now live with and beyond their grief. They must now live well without you. There may be facets of the service that you would not have thought to include, things that need to be said to strengthen the resolve of those whom you loved, so that they are more fitted to continue living carefully and lovingly. Give your family room to say what needs to be said and to do what needs to be done. It is your funeral, but they are also participants. For this reason it may be important not to prepare your own funeral service.

Being truthful, open and upfront are also important. It is absolutely not helpful to say fine religious things about someone who never saw inside a church door. It's just as unhelpful to talk about a loving wife and partner if the one deceased was an overbearing, dominant person. It is equally unhelpful to be blunt and critical with words that will hurt family feelings, rather than offer support and comfort.

Have everything in order before you die. It is helpful to tell your family what your wishes are. It is also important to make write a 'Last Will and Testament.' A Will can be any written expression of your wishes that has been signed by you, your signature being witnessed by two others. Your

Will usually appoints trustees who will see that your wishes are carried out in terms of your Will. Often trustees are members of your family or your close friends. Where there is considerable finance, property or business involved, it is prudent to have a solicitor draw up your Will. Simple Wills can be lodged with the Public Trustee. There will be small costs involved for these services. If you do not write a Will your family may have to wait several months before your estate can be settled, and your partner may suffer financial hardship during that time. There is a process for the Coroner and the courts to follow for those who die without a Will. It is good practice to get a Will written within a week of your marriage, and to update your Will each time you have a child, shift house or when family circumstances change.

Wills can be very simple or highly complicated. A simple Will may just state that your property is to be divided equally among your family after your partner, who may outlive you, has died. A complicated Will may state in detail who is to get what: the rocking chair, grandma's vase, etc. Such complicated detail can be avoided if you have talked with your family about your wishes, and trust the details to them. Sometimes older people leave a name on the bottom of each article indicating who is to be gifted that article. You can, of course, begin giving your valued treasures away before you die.

Don't assume that Dad will die first, just because men have a slightly shorter life expectancy than women. And don't underestimate the feeling of loneliness that will engulf your life when your partner departs. Grief and bereavement are a necessary healing process to pass through when someone you loved is no longer an active part of your daily life. (That applies to separation and divorce also.) I recall vividly my elderly mother saying to me as we walked hand in hand, "You will never know how lonely I have been since Alan died." Grief can remain for years, forever, and can creep up suddenly and be upon us each time we are reminded of the love we shared and enjoyed. Grief also includes the painful process of adjusting to new circumstances and opportunities. It has within it the potential for hopefulness and renewal.

Wisdom prompts us to think ahead about some of the practical results of your partner dying. Make sure that you have bank accounts that the remaining partner can access and operate. Give your partner the opportunity to carry on with the daily management of their life. Arrange for a Joint Power Of Attorney agreement. This will provide the surviving spouse/ partner continued access to joint banking facilities.

Let's talk briefly about funeral costs. Funeral directors tell me that the current cost of a simple funeral is about $7,500 for a cremation and $13,000 for a burial. There are a range of options and costs. This cost represents a significant amount that must be allowed for in your budget or savings. If you forget to budget for this 'one-off, final cost' your surviving partner, or your family, are going to be left significantly out of pocket.

Alternatively, you can arrange for a prepaid funeral account with your chosen funeral company. This may involve regular small payments into a funeral account. The Funeral Directors Association of NZ will be able to give you details. They have a very helpful booklet on all aspects of funeral arrangements, available from your local funeral company.

Funeral costs are likely to include:

- The purchase of a burial plot or the cost of cremation.
- The undertaker's fees.
- A casket.
- Catering for the reception following the service.
- For a church funeral, the cost may include fees for the minister, the organist and using the church.
- Newspaper advertisements.
- Transport arrangements for the family.
- Accommodation of close family and relatives.
- Floral arrangements.

There is a Death and Funeral Benefit available through Work and Income NZ This may be of considerable assistance.

Many of the funeral details can be decided well in advance. If this is done it relieves family from the need to make sudden arrangements within a limited time frame when their loved one dies. Thus family are free to spend quality time together sharing their grief, their family story, their support and their love. That is, after all, what is really important.

Attitude

Some years ago I attended the annual meeting of the Wanganui Senior Citizens Association. Elizabeth Nobel, the chairwoman, a much respected city counsellor, suddenly paused half way through presenting her annual report, smiled and announced, "Oh, look at that, I have put my cardigan on inside out." All those attending the meeting had a good laugh and we then continued with the meeting.

Being able to smile and joke about our own misadventures is a sign of maturity. It is a sign of some depth of character that we are able to laugh at ourselves.

Smiling and laughing is apparently one of those qualities that keeps us young and some research indicates that it also contributes to our good health and longevity. It reflects a positive attitude to life, a desire to look for the best in life. But laughter resulting from a desire to be the centre of attention can also mask the inner sadness that we often feel, but desperately try to find ways of hiding. Sometimes we feel unsafe about revealing our true self. It is easy to live behind a mask. Each of us needs an inner group of friends and family, with whom we can feel confident enough to be ourselves, to take the mask off and know that we will be accepted.

Sometimes I play a game to imagine how happy people really are. As people walk towards me, will they smile, nod a greeting and look me in the eye? The game assumes that if you are happy you can comfortably look others in the eye as they pass by. Try it. You will find that many people quickly turn their gaze away, while self confident people often return a nod or a smile to acknowledge your unspoken greeting. I am quick to add that I have no scientific basis for what are really my personal assumptions. Try it, it's fun. Years ago, while walking through Cathedral Square in Christchurch, I was indulging in this trivia, when my smile was returned by a longtime friend walking towards me. We had a great conversation.

Not everyone has a joyous view of life. My hospital chaplaincy work as a hospital visitor often reminded me that there are many people who have been dealt a raw deal in life. Illness, accident and broken relationships all come into this category. Sometimes a less than positive experience is of our own making. It also follows that if we got ourselves into a messy corner we probably have the ability to get ourselves out again. But sometimes we do need help out of the doldrums. At other times the best we can do is to grin and bear it, forgiving those who have hurt us. It is also possible that if we learn from the hurts we will grow a little.

I have come to understand that there are two sorts of people. There are those who rise above disappointing, tragic, life-distorting and destroying moments, learning from the experience. And there are those who cling to the hurt, travel with it and allow it to warp and fill their lives with a pain that colours everything they do. Put another way: there are those who shape life and those who let life shape them.

Many older people who experienced the World Wars and the Great Depression, came through with the attitude that, "Never again would they let this happen." They journeyed, adventured, took risks, bought, sold and built, determined to creatively shape a more positive world. Then there were those, not a few of them, who kept their hurts to themselves; never risked their livelihood by putting a foot wrong; kept their money safe in a bank instead of investing it in the developing world around them; did what was necessary to be a responsible neighbour, but never truly became a good neighbour. They survived, but never lived abundantly and creatively. Wars and depressions are painful, but it is possible to live beyond them, learning their lessons and, out of the rubble, to shape new dreams.

I was brought up in Christchurch. Post-earthquake Christchurch is not the city I once knew. Those memories will never be possible again. But out of the pain of destruction a new city will rise, bringing to life new dreams, new shapes and new possibilities. That is why rebuilding a traditionally shaped Cathedral as the central symbol of Christchurch life will, if it happens, be a backward facing statement and not in tune with the spirit of rebuilding and renewal. It is not preserved or revived tradition that Christchurch needs, but a creative future.

Some years ago my youngest brother contracted a bone cancer in his upper leg and his leg had to be amputated. I recall how he shared with me that, by living one day at a time, he had found a positive way through that painful, life changing experience. His story reminded me of some of the words of Jesus, "Take no thought for tomorrow, tomorrow will take care of itself." It is not an easy ride to live one day at a time looking for each positive moment.

I have some daily routines. When I rise, I stretch and open the curtains to let in the light. Then I have a shower and let the warmth of the water flow over me and into me. While this is happening I set myself one or two tasks to complete throughout that day. By the time I am dry I have shaped some positive goals for the day. These goals may or may not be achieved that day. Achieving my goal is not the point, it is the planning ahead, and the steps taken towards the goal that satisfy. Often the goal remains to be fulfilled another day. To satisfactorily reach my goal is an added bonus. Over breakfast I check my diary for family events, grandchildren's birthdays, etc. and often find that I have forgotten that some other activity must be included. Consequently an adjustment to the first goals set may be necessary. Often this adjustment is the result of my wife jogging my memory. Quite regularly, today's goals will not be met until tomorrow.

After each day, when evening comes, many people find it helpful to briefly review the activities and achievements of that day. I like to be able to say to myself, something positive was achieved; a project has been completed; a friendship shared; a new piece of knowledge gained. And as I drift off to sleep, I find myself saying, "Thank you God for the snippet of life we shared today, thank you." And as an afterthought, "Please, if time permits, give me one more joyous day tomorrow."

Love and sexuality

"Love is patient, love is kind; love is not envious or boastful or arrogant or rude. It does not insist on its own way; it is not irritable or resentful; it does not rejoice in wrongdoing, but rejoices in the truth. Love bears all things, believes all things, hopes all things, endures all things. Love never ends." *1 Corinthians 13:4-8.*

"O that you would kiss me with the kisses of your mouth! Your love is better than wine. There is a fragrance about you. I have entered my garden, my sweetheart, my bride. I am gathering my spices and myrrh. Let me hear your voice from the garden my love. Make haste, my beloved, and be like a little gazelle or a young stag upon the mountains where the spices grow." *Song of Solomon.*

Following World War II, the modern, free world in which we live took shape. Men and women returning from war service, in Europe and the Pacific, were determined to build the ideals they had fought for into the culture in which they lived. They had found plenty of time in the trenches to debate and shape new dreams. They dreamt of home and family, the acquisition of education, the creative ability that would flow from that knowledge and the freedom to choose their own directions in life. These would become the measures by which people lived. And live they did.

As well, there was a desire to put the experience of war — its hurt, destruction and guilt — behind and to get on with the job of building the modern scientific age. The religious and moral boundaries of the past were shaken off, trashed, discarded, thrown out, and replaced by freedom of choice without fear, something never experienced before.

Those who had delayed courtship and marriage during the war years now renewed their love. They set about having a family and populated the country with a generation of fun loving, pleasure seeking children. Within a generation these post-war children grew to hold central in their lives their ability to make personal moral and sexual choices of their own.

One of the great inventions of this age of personal knowledge and experience was the invention of effective contraceptive devices. The contraceptive pill became part of the daily life of couples, including Roman

Catholic parents, even though the Catholic Church strongly opposed, and still does, anything that interfered with natural procreation. This was deemed God's sphere of activity, not to be meddled with by any man or woman.

The results of this sexual freedom were many. Women were now able to make personal choices about their sexuality and pregnancy. Teens began experimenting with sex at a younger age. The incidence of sexually transmitted disease, brought home by returned soldiers, increased greatly. Growing teens and young adults refused to listen to the traditional advice of their parents because it was guidance for a generation that no longer held the same morality and dreams. And the population boomed.

A major consequence of this sexual revolution, for that is what it was, was release from the fear of unwanted pregnancies. Sex became a joyous experience. Life was to be celebrated. Sex is now about sharing the deepest moments of personal enjoyment. The end result of sexual intercourse shifted from procreation, having children, to the enjoyment of life.

Those of us between 60 and 75 years of age are the children of the post-war baby boom. We were the first generation to be cultured within this post-war freedom. As a result we take sexual freedom and pleasure as our right. We have been infused with the desire to stay young and sexually active as long as we choose.

The world of advertising and entertainment continues to give the impression that we live in a young people's world. Such advertising sells products and makes money. This focus on youthfulness continues in developing countries where the average age is often under 20. But it is not so noticeable in New Zealand where population statistics indicate that 635,000 (14% of the population) are over 65 and that 97% of them are on National Superannuation. Indeed, declining numbers in the work force threaten continued government support for welfare programmes.

For seniors who grew up in a sexually open society there is a question to answer: what place does sexual morality, that has moved from child bearing priorities to an emphasis on sexual pleasure, have in the life of those over 60? In a very individualist culture that is a question for each person to answer.

This youth orientated culture, particularly its media celebrities and the advertising machine which finances and encourages everything youthful, continues to blare out its message: dress young, make up young, speak young, walk young, keep yourself sexually young, don't admit you are anything but young. But the aching joints of our bodies and the time that it now takes to complete simple daily physical tasks; the number of pills we take morning and evening; and the fact that we drop off to sleep watching television, and again as soon as we get into bed; these seem to be saying, slow down, have a rest, eat less fast food, watch your diet, don't worry about having less powerful sexual orgasms; you are getting old.

The truth is that we are getting old. We do slow down in physical activity, including sexual activity. But a hug and a kiss before we drop off to sleep are just as meaningful, if not more so, in old age than they ever were before. It takes just the touch of a hand around the waist, a touch on an arm, or an arm resting on a shoulder, to express that love which has been maturing for many years. In the first flush of our courtship, engagement and marriage, it was each orgasmic moment which was both momentous and meaningful. That was the experience we needed and sought when we were young. In old age, years of togetherness bring an experience of sexuality that no longer depends upon the mountain top orgasm to express the inner love between partners that has been there throughout long years of loving.

Let me state it clearly and bluntly, sex is not just about the orgasm experience. Sex in old age, and I suspect it is the same in each stage of our development, is about every word, every act of friendship and love, every knowing whisper, every quick smile and every glance across a crowed room to catch your significant other's loving eye. It is about walking on the beach hand in hand. It is about baking a batch of muffins as a surprise. It is about picking the first flower in the garden as a gift for the one you love. It is about laughing together and crying together. Sexuality is about saying, "This TV programme is the pits, lets go to bed."

Dreaming sensibly

"An eighty year old Japanese mountain climber, who has had heart surgery four times, is heading to Mount Everest to try for a third accent of the world's highest peak. He would become the oldest person to reach the top if he succeeds. Yuichiro Miura climbed to the summit of the 8850m mountain in 2003 and 2008. He skied down Everest from an altitude of 8000m in 1970." *Reuters report 3 March 2013.*

How often have you heard the saying, "Age is no barrier?" We live in a day and age when it is quite common to live well into the 80s and 90s. When we were children the average life expectancy was about 70 years. In Biblical times it was considered that, "the days of our lives are seventy years, or perhaps eighty if we are strong" (Psalm 90:10). Longevity used to be equated with wisdom; elders were sought out and listened to for their experience and good advice. The same applies today for Maori elders. How the world has changed. The last two decades of our life are now, more often than not, seen as an opportunity to fulfil long held dreams of activities long since postponed for lack of time or money, or dreams bypassed when life took a different direction. Dreams to travel; the dream to build a boat and sail the world; to succeed as an Olympian; to make a million; these are the dreams of young people who have time and physical fitness on their side. Few of those over 60 have the energy to climb their Everest.

But there may still be some mountains that we are able to climb. Many Australians have a retirement dream to drive 14,000km right around their island continent. They have earned the nick name, 'grey nomads.' I have known people whose dream was to walk from North Cape to Bluff. Some years ago I heard the story of a little old lady who every two years packed all she needed in a trunk and went off to visit all her relatives. It is not unheard of for a retired person to follow their dream to start and succeed in building the business they always wanted to operate.

One way to view our senior years is to see them as an opportunity given to us so that we may have time to follow through on our most compelling dreams. First let me share a few cautionary words. Some dreams are unrealistic, they are dreams and will always remain dreams. You may find that your childhood ambition is too costly. My dream to build a 30 foot ketch was such a dream. At 60 plus you probably do not have the energy and fitness required to scale Mt Cook. These dreams were for our adolescence and our young adulthood. Or perhaps they were for our family life and our children. Our children have long since begun following their own dreams. Perhaps it is time those earlier dreams became prayers that shape new, more suitable ambitions.

But dreaming is not all disappointment. The good news is that many of our dreams are realistic. If you have the money, travel the world. You have always wanted to climb the Remarkables. Visit the Pyramids. Go hunt elephants. That was the joyful slogan we shared with our family and friends as we set off to live in the United Kingdom in 1997. Hunting elephants meant for us, explore Europe and take whatever opportunities travel gave. We saw our first elephant in Bangkok, Thailand on our way home. I recall it was evening coming on darkness and there he was, an elephant wandering along the street with a tail-light strapped to his tail.

Go for it. Open your café. Buy that bright yellow sports car, but make sure your arthritic joints allow you not only to get into the drivers seat, but also to get out again. Build your dream home. Organise the family reunion you have always talked about. My round-the-world 30 foot ketch has been scaled down to become a one metre radio controlled sail boat. It took over four years to complete. Dreams are worth having even if they need to be reshaped along the way. There is another powerful reshaping tool that accompanies old age, the wisdom of one's husband or wife. That comes with a more realistic approach to encouragement and a willingness to accept sound advice.

If you have a partner, share and encourage their dream. The end result is often more creative and enjoyable.

How do you work through the dreams that your family may have for you? Adult children do share ideas and grizzles about their parents, and they do come up with 'creative' suggestions as to how we should be living. It is great that our children are so concerned for our well-being. But it's a good idea for family to discuss their concerns with us before they become hard and fast 'this is what has to happen' proposals. I've lost count of the number of times that I have heard grown children proposing that it is time to pencil Mum in for a pensioner's unit at the old people's home; or commenting, "Dad's driving is becoming so erratic that I wonder if I should talk with the traffic department before he takes his 75 year driving test." There have been times when I have wanted to scream, "It is not your responsibility to decide what your parents should or should not do." Aged parents are quite capable of making their own decisions.

However, there are some circumstances when you will not be capable of deciding for yourself. Someone else should have a key to your house and be able to check on you if no one has seen you up and about for a few days. Alternatively, arrange with your neighbour that, if you do not have the lounge curtains drawn my 9am, they should phone your daughter. A good neighbour should have your family contact phone numbers. At the very least someone should know where you keep a spare key. It is a good idea to arrange to talk with someone at a set time each day, and if you have not rung they know to check you out.

When you travel and are away from home for any length of time, you should arrange for someone to empty your letterbox. A bulging letterbox is an advertisement to any light-fingered passerby that your house is empty. Have a neighbour park their car in your drive. Buy an automatic timer switch that turns on a light in the lounge every evening, then off again at your normal bed time. If you are on an extended trip it may be wise to give one of your family Enduring Power of Attorney, so they have the ability to operate your bank account, write cheques on your behalf and make sure that your monthly accounts are not overdue.

There are also some medical circumstances when it is wise to have given someone an Enduring Power of Attorney. If you have had a serious stroke you may no longer be able to transact business. An accident may leave you incapacitated for a long period. Hopefully none of these will happen to you, but as the Boy Scouts' motto concisely states, "Be Prepared." You probably need to talk with your solicitor before signing Enduring Power of Attorney papers. At the very least, talk with all your children and immediate family about your wishes.

Perhaps the best you can do is pass your dream on to the next generation. In European society, businesses, family fortunes and responsibilities were commonly passed to the oldest son. Thus several generations often carried the family dream to fruition. This is one of the ways in which our culture has progressed its ideals and values.

Talk with your children. Share with them the ambitions and convictions that you hold in your heart. Give them the chance to hold the dream in their hearts.

Ageism and discrimination

A story shared by a hospital patient. "I'm not looking forward to this afternoon. My daughter has arrived from Australia and will be in to visit me. I'm a bit anxious. I know what she will want. She wants me to go and live with her in Sydney. I don't want to move away from all my friends. They all live here. And this is where my memories are. Jim and I built our first home in Tauranga. We were so happy there. We lived very happily together. I don't want to leave all that behind." *Lucy D.*

There is a characteristic quality of parenting that we need to take seriously. Parents are ultimately responsible for the decisions and directions of their family. We spend 20 years instilling that into the minds of our children. It should not be surprising that, when they become adults responsible for their own children, they want to exercise that responsibility themselves. Neither should it surprise us that, when our children see their parents aging and becoming less capable of meeting all the daily demands of living in their own homes, often alone, they want to assist us to make sensible decisions, sometimes making decisions for us. We may see it as our children taking over our lives, and resent the intrusion. The roles somehow get reversed. Children often want to tell aging parents what to do and how to live.

"Come and live with us Mum. We have the spare room." No one wants to move away from the family home.

"I'll order meals on wheels for you." Try saying that to a proud cook to see what response you get.

"Dad you really must get rid of all this old china that you and Mum had. You only need a couple of settings now." Perhaps it's the last of the wedding gift china and carries deep memories.

"You don't need a large garden now. I'll get my Jim to put it down in grass." Producing fresh vegetables was probably an essential part of daily family life, enjoyed with pride and satisfaction.

Renewing a driving license, moving out of the family home into a unit, looking for a suitable retirement village, the cleanliness of the house, not taking the tablets prescribed, getting the lawns mowed, the house needing painting — there are a host of flash points that can cause substantial worry for both older people and their anxious caring families.

As we age we may become upset with those whom we love who, with genuine concern, make what they consider to be helpful suggestions. We get upset for two reasons. One, it's our children telling us what to do. Two, we don't want to admit to our children that there are some things that we no longer do well. We don't want to let our children know that our pride is being hurt a little.

If we expect our children to offer us enough space to make our own decisions, perhaps we should reciprocate a little and listen to their concerns. Maybe we could share ideas and look for a more positive way forward as a solution that we can all own. No one said it would be easy.

The reality of aging is that we do slow down, we are growing old, and we no longer have the energy we need to get things done as efficiently as we used to. Perhaps our eyesight is failing and our hearing may also be declining. We have to be honest and open, often when we least wish to be. And we don't like to admit that our children may actually know more about some aspect of life than we do.

There is another expression of ageism that can be quite frightening. It is the way in which a small minority of retailers and tradespeople take advantage of older people. Door-to-door salespeople may expect homeowners to make on-the-spot decisions. Older people, particularly older women living alone, often find themselves pressured into making a decision, "Today." "If you buy today a 20% discount applies." Sometimes information is withheld or lacking. Often the right of consumers to a ten day cooling off clause is not explained. Door-to-door salespeople typify this form of abuse.

There are those outside the family who may take advantage of older people, treating them as objects who cannot make their own decisions. "Your trees need a trim." "Your gutters need leaf excluders." "Now this car is a little gem and it should meet all your round town needs." Claims may be made that you have not been aware of and which you cannot check out for yourself, right there and then. You feel hassled into making a quick decision. Ask for some written material so that you can have time to make a decision. Given time, check out the claims being made. Do you need the service? And just as important, can you meet the cost?

It's not truly an example of ageism, but watch out for legalese; language that you do not fully understand. And this applies not only to senior people but to all people. We may receive correspondence from businesses and Government Departments that is full of jargon. Accounting departments are good at disguising the calculations that lead to the bottom line fact that you owe them money. I imagine that they aim to get your payment as promptly and painlessly as possible.

Solicitors and Government Departments sometimes use language that is incomprehensible. Some years ago, just before I retired, I received NZ Accident Compensation payments fortnightly. The payment statement always said, "Abatement payment." I looked up the word in a dictionary and found it meant, 'to make or become less in amount.' I enquired of my ACC manager what it meant and I am no wiser. I still have no idea how that meaning refers to a fortnightly payment. Thankfully the payments kept arriving. Be sure that you understand what advertising, financial and legal language is actually saying. Be careful to read the small print that details the conditions under which you have purchased goods and services.

One final comment regarding ageism. There is a very special relationship between old people, their families and their communities. When that relationship is expressed carefully, when someone opens a door to let you enter first, when a child passes you the chocolates before sharing them with others in the room, when you are asked to say the grace at a family meal; you will know that your age is honoured and respected. I do not have a driver's licence so I often ride on buses. Regularly when the bus is full, a young person will stand and offer me a seat. The first time it happened I was offered a seat by a young woman. All my upbringing had taught me to stand for women. I felt that I should stand for her. She insisted that I take her seat and I realised it was an honour to be respected for my age. There is an ageism that treats you as an honoured and respected member of society.

Old, old age

I knew Annie when she was about 60 and I was a small child. I thought she was old then. Annie was a member of our church and a close friend of my grandmother. Annie lived by herself, her husband Frank had died when he was 50. She rode her old bike everywhere. Often Annie visited her friends late in the afternoon in the hope that they would invite her to stay for the evening meal. 40 years later when I became her parish minister Annie was still riding her bike and visiting her friends. I recall visiting Annie one afternoon. I could hear her talking and I found her in her back garden. I thought that she was talking to herself about the beauty of the flowers but, after being startled when she realised that someone was behind her, she confessed that she was saying her prayers. I learnt she often talked to her Lord in the garden. Annie gave up riding her bike and visiting her friends when she was 99. At age 100 years and 5 days Annie died. We celebrated her life with thanksgiving.

I was so pleased that I was Annie's minister. I felt that in being her pastor I was able to give back something of the care and inspiration that I had received from her and other members of the parish in which I grew up. I was surprised that Annie was still, at age 100, sharing her gifts of life with me and with those around her.

In 2007, when I retired from full time work, I accepted a part time Hospital Chaplaincy appointment, one day a week. Each Tuesday I travelled across the city to Wesley Hospital to be chaplain to a number of older people, many with Alzheimer's disease. I counted it a privilege to work with the staff and patients. There were two patients who had reached the age of 100.

Having been away from active on-the-ward chaplaincy for about six years I decided to read widely about old age. I found to my surprise, that Shakespeare's 'seven ages of man' — the stages of human development outline which had been adopted for use by the educational world as a framework to describe child and human development, and which had been drilled into me so thoroughly as a teacher trainee many years before — had become, 'the eight stages of human development.'

A new category, 'old, old age' had been added. Given that the average life expectancy in developed countries has, since the World Wars, risen from 70 to the mid-80s, and that many people are living to be 90 plus, and a few to over 100, it seems logical to add another stage describing this senior elders group.

Like every stage of human development, it is characterised as a time to adjust to the demands and expectations of that age. The over 60 years offer us time to do those things that we have dreamt of doing all our lives. The 75 plus years offer us another chance, often with some supporting help from family and friends, to shape our lives into a quality package.

Let's put it another way, our senior years give us time and space to hone our friendships and our philosophy of life, but 80 plus gives the opportunity to polish the person that we, through our own choices, have become.

Don't just let it happen, because it won't. Drifting along, hoping life will all fall into place, is a sure recipe for a life that lurches from one problem to another. Rather, plan to make quality living happen and it will. My Mum was a good cook, but as she aged she relied upon her memory for the details of the recipe. Consequently, sometimes the bread didn't rise or the biscuits lacked flavour. Her Anzac biscuits never turned out the same as the previous batch, though strangely they always tasted good. To shape life well you have to follow the recipe. But unlike baking, you become personally involved with the significant others in your life who share your beliefs and culture in writing the recipe. Quality living is not individual, it is corporate. During your life you do have the chance to share in writing the script of the recipe. To get full flavour and texture and good nourishment, dream the recipe and follow the dream.

Laugh at life, enjoy life, it is meant to be abundant with pleasure. In spite of ill health, and often lacking in financial richness, life can be full to overflowing with satisfaction and laughter. Old, old age is meant to be fun.

Essentially my life's work has been about communicating what I hope is good news. Television advertisements have interested me for a long time because they are about communication. They are short, concise messages surrounded by attractive pictures, graphics, words and music. They are often crafted around a short story and try to sell you one central message, in the hope that you will purchase the product. There is an advertisement for cheese in which an old man shares his love for cheese making and mature cheese with his grandson. The punch line is, "Good things take time."

Make sure that you are on to a good thing and give yourself enough time to shape your retirement well. Your old age and old, old age are worth it. Enjoy the 60 70 80 90 years.

Organisations Working with Older People

60 Up

www.60supmovement.org.nz

Social support and services for those over 60.

Aged Concern

www.ageconcern.co.nz

For your local branch see Yellow Pages.

Budget Advice Services

Freephone 0508 BUDGETLINE (283 438)

Help with planning your weekly budget.

Diabetes NZ

www.diabetes.org.nz

Support for those with Diabetes. Also consult your local medical centre.

Senior Net

www.seniornet.org.nz

Training in the use of computer skills.

Royal New Zealand Foundation of the Blind

www.rnzfb.org.nz

Support services for sight impaired people.

Funeral Directors Association of NZ

www.funeralsnewzealand.co.nz

See also your local Yellow Pages.

Grey Power

www.greypower.co.nz

Social and political support for seniors.

Guide To Retirement

www.guidetoretirement.co.nz

Post: PO Box 303244, North Harbour, 0751

Phone: 09 281 4550

Heart Foundation

www.heartfoundation.org.nz

Freephone: 0800 863 375

Support and training for those with cardiac illness.

Office of Senior Citizens. Te Tari Kaumatua

Administered by the Ministry of Social Development.

www.msd.govt.nz

Freephone 0800 273 674

Older Peoples' Statistics. NZ Government.

www.stats.govt.nz

Public Trustee

www.publictrust.co.nz

Freehone 0800 371 471, Free fax 0800 371 001

Relationship Services

Assistance with relationships and marriage guidance. See your local Yellow Pages.

WINZ. Work and Income Services

Seniors Services Freephone 0800 552 002

New Zealand Superannuation support.

Index

St John's Ambulance 42, 49
storage room 18
stories 5, 25

T

tax refund 32
taxation 32
Te Tari Kaumatua 73
telephone applications 31, 46
telephone directories 46
telephones 29
tiled flooring 18
toilets 17
traffic noise 14
transport 9, 11, 14, 37, 42, 54
travel 8, 11, 13–14, 16, 23, 25,
    28, 38, 57, 62–64, 69
travel precautions 23
TV advertisements 39, 70

V

values 22, 25–26, 47, 65
vegetable garden 16, 19, 21, 35

W

wall space 14, 19
washing lines 19
washing powder 31
Wesley Hospital, Auckland 69
wet rooms 15, 18
wheel chair access 18
wills 53
WINZ. Work and Income Services 74
wisdom 4, 26, 53, 62–63
World Wars 57, 70

60 70 80 90

www.ingramcontent.com/pod-product-compliance
Lightning Source LLC
Chambersburg PA
CBHW050602280326
41933CB00011B/1944